The Styer-Fitzgerald
Program for Functional
Academics

Teacher's Guide to
Peer Tutoring

Secondary Level

Created by

CANDICE STYER, Ph.D.

AND

SUZANNE FITZGERALD, M.Ed.

Published by

Specially Designed
Education Services

The Styer-Fitzgerald Program for Functional Academics
Teacher's Guide to Peer Tutoring

Second Edition
First U.S. Edition Published in 2015

SPECIALLY DESIGNED EDUCATION SERVICES
18223 102ND AVE NE
SUITE B
BOTHELL, WA 98011

www.SDESworks.com

ISBN 978-0-9969130-4-1

Cover Design by

hewitt
by design

www.hewittbydesign.com

A big thank you to our editor extraordinaire, Debbie Austin.

Website URLs are provided as resource references. The publisher does not maintain these sites, all of which were active and valid at the time of publication. Please note that over time, URLs and/or their content may change. We regret any inconvenience this may cause readers.

*Microsoft and Word are either registered trademarks or trademarks of Microsoft Corporation in the United States and/or other countries.
All other company, product, and service names mentioned herein may be
registered trademarks, trademarks, or service marks of their respective holders.*

Printed by CreateSpace, An Amazon.com Company

TABLE OF CONTENTS

A COPY OF THE PEER TUTOR STUDENT HANDBOOK IS INCLUDED AT THE END OF THIS GUIDE

Introduction to Peer Tutoring

This teaching guide is designed to help you implement and maintain a successful peer tutoring program. As you read, it will be helpful for you to refer to the *Peer Tutor Student Handbook** so you can see relevant information from your peer tutor's viewpoint. The *Peer Tutor Student Handbook* is included at the end of this guide.

Peer tutors are general education students (usually secondary level) who help as teaching assistants in both elementary and secondary special education classrooms. To have a successful peer tutor program, you need to recruit students who are dedicated and dependable, exhibit a positive attitude, and who have the desire to help others. After recruiting and selecting students for your peer tutoring program, you will need to train them, monitor their progress, manage their schedules, address challenges, and evaluate their efforts.

Because each special education classroom is different—serving varied student populations with a broad spectrum of disabilities—it becomes important for you to tailor your peer tutoring program to meet the specific needs of your students. The ideas in this guide are suggestions for your peer tutoring program. Use the suggestions that best apply to your classroom and situation with the understanding that over time and with new students, those needs can change. Here are some tips for keeping your peer tutoring program current:

- Refresh your program by rereading this guide periodically and by keeping abreast of the things other teachers are doing that might also work for you.

- Visit the Freebies page on the Styer-Fitzgerald website (www.styer-fitzgerald.com) to find beneficial materials available as free downloads for teachers to use in their Functional Academics classrooms as well as with their peer tutoring programs.

- Use resources found in other websites and publications. Here are a couple to get you started:

  - www.kypeertutoring.org
  - www.wsdsonline.org/video-library/deaf-blind-videos/peer-programs/ (Washington Sensory Disabilities Services)

*Note: Each peer tutor needs a copy of the *Peer Tutor Student Handbook* available from Amazon.com, CreateSpace.com, and other retail outlets.

Benefits of a Successful Peer Tutoring Program

The benefits of a peer tutoring program are numerous. Those who participate in a peer tutor program gain experiences that have a long-lasting impact. In some cases the experience is life-altering for everyone involved—for students with disabilities, for the typically developing peers who serve as their tutors, and for special education teachers.

Benefits to Students with Disabilities

For students with disabilities, the peer connection affords them the opportunity to learn and practice appropriate social skills. The social skills that special education students learn from their typically developing peers are the very skills they need in order to fully participate in their communities. The relationships between peer tutors and special education students provide a more realistic model of the types of behaviors expected outside of self-contained classrooms.

Working with peer tutors provides additional opportunities for students with disabilities to develop friendships with those to whom they might not otherwise have access. These relationships often result in increased self-esteem and empathy on the part of both the students with disabilities and their tutors.

Benefits to Peer Tutors

For the general education students—the peer tutors—there are numerous rewards for working with students who have disabilities. The primary benefit is the opportunity to understand and have empathy for people who are different from themselves and at the same time observe and appreciate the special education students' similarities to themselves.

At a time when many teenagers become self-involved, working with students who have challenges often can be enlightening and life-altering. Personal satisfaction and increased confidence are natural outcomes for general education students who participate in peer tutoring programs within their school community.

For tutors who are interested in careers in the helping professions such as social work and teaching, tutoring provides the opportunity to explore the field of education and determine if it is a good fit. Additionally, the peer tutor experience makes a powerful promotional statement on college applications and job résumés.

Benefits to Teachers

By having well-trained peer tutors in their classrooms, special education teachers find they have more flexible schedules. This then increases a teacher's opportunity to provide one-to-one instruction to the special education students who require it the most.

You can also have peer tutors work with your students outside the special education classroom as mentors in general education classes. Use your tutors in classes such as PE, computer programming, art, or French. Tutors can also help students work at vocational training sites on campus such as the library, counseling office, and attendance office.

Bringing students with disabilities together with their peers who do not have disabilities is a win-win situation for everyone involved.

Recruiting Peer Tutors

If you are just beginning to design a peer tutoring program, try any or all of these ideas, expanding and relying on the ones that work best for you. If you already have peer tutors and are looking for more, try the recruiting suggestions in this section that you think might help your program. These can be used in addition to the recruiting tools you found to be successful in the past.

As mentioned in the Introduction, your program will be most successful when you find general education students who are dedicated and dependable, who exhibit a positive attitude, and who have the desire to help others.

- You can often spot students who have a helping nature by observing the natural interactions of general education students with your special education students. When you see those sorts of positive interactions, invite the general education student to visit your classroom.

- Find those general education students who might be struggling with academics. They can benefit by practicing their own skills as they tutor your students with disabilities. For example, a general education eighth grader who is not yet reading at grade level can gain skill and confidence by reading to your students who read at a lower grade level.

Involve Your School Community

Gaining the support of the school community—those outside your classroom such as other teachers, administrators, the principal, and the parents of your students—will help ensure the success of your peer tutors and your program.

- Inform the parents of your students about your peer tutoring program. Keeping them informed will help them understand the efficacy of having peer tutors in the classroom.

- You will need to obtain permission from the parents of your students in order to disclose information about specific students and their disabilities. Your students' peers are naturally curious about the disabilities of your class members. Your ability to discuss specific disabilities of particular students with your peer tutors can go a long way toward promoting understanding and empathy. A sample permission form is included in Appendix A and is also provided on the Freebies page of the Styer-Fitzgerald website (www.styer-fitzgerald.com) to download and modify if desired.

- Gain support from your principal, counselors, and administrators by meeting with them to ask about the process you need to go through to set up a peer tutoring program at your school. Principals and other administrators can be instrumental in assisting you to set up credit for your tutors. They can also aid and support your effort with recruiting. Ask administrators to allow time at staff meetings for you to discuss your program. It might be helpful to provide them with a copy of the *Peer Tutor Student Handbook* as well as the peer tutor application and teacher reference form found in Appendix A. These forms are also available on the Freebies page of the Styer-Fitzgerald website (www.styer-fitzgerald.com) to download and modify if desired.

- Take opportunities at staff meetings to share details about your peer tutor program and ask teachers for permission to present information to their general education classes. If general education teachers are supportive of your efforts, they can become excellent recruiters for your program. Additionally, it can be helpful to hold a meeting or give a presentation about your students and disability awareness for other teachers and staff members and allow opportunities for questions. Many adults are unsure how to interact and support students with severe disabilities.

Activities and Ideas for Recruiting

To boost your recruiting efforts, use some of these ideas or build on them to suit your needs. Be sure to state the steps students need to take in order to become peer tutors (listed below).

- In morning announcements, include a pitch about peer tutoring opportunities. Be sure to let students know whom to see if they are interested. For example:

  "Change a life! Make a difference! Become a Peer Tutor in the Functional Academics life skills program! Next year, the Functional Academics special education program is recruiting peer tutors to assist our students with disabilities in areas of academics, social skills, and daily living skills. If you are interested in becoming a Peer Tutor, or would like more information, please see _____ in Room _____."

- Create a poster or visual display to place outside your classroom. Make it colorful and informative to catch the attention of general education peers and let them know you are recruiting. See a sample on the Freebies page of the Styer-Fitzgerald website (www.styer-fitzgerald.com).

- Make recruitment flyers and have your students distribute them during lunch hour, recess, or passing periods.

- Find teachers who understand your peer tutor program—teachers who "get it." Send emails to those teachers and ask them to schedule some time (perhaps fifteen or twenty minutes) for you to make a presentation to their students, either by yourself or with some of your current peer tutors.

  - If you make the presentation by yourself, tell students about your class. Elaborate about what you do with your students (Functional Academics/life skills). Explain your goals for your special education students—for example, independence. Give examples of how tutors play a significant role in assisting your students to reach those goals—for instance, by having peer tutors teach students to tell time or by helping special education students by taking notes in general education classes.

  - If you have current peer tutors, invite them to help make presentations. Because students gain more confidence or find comfort by having others with them, invite more than one peer tutor. You might try forming a panel of three peer tutors who can present as opportunities arise. After giving a brief description of your special education class, students, and curriculum, allow each tutor a couple of minutes to speak. Have the tutors explain their reasons for becoming involved in the program, the challenges they have faced, and what they have gained from their experiences.

Steps Students Can Take to Become Peer Tutors

These are the steps commonly taken by students who want to participate in a peer tutoring program. Use the steps that apply to your situation or add other steps as necessary. Students should:

1. Meet with you (the special education teacher) and complete an application. See a sample Peer Tutor Application in Appendix A. A modifiable version is available on the Freebies page of the Styer-Fitzgerald

website (www.styer-fitzgerald.com). Keep 5-10 applications on hand and accessible for you and your staff to give to potential tutors.

2. Provide a letter of recommendation or reference from two teachers. See a sample Peer Tutor Reference Form in Appendix A. A modifiable version is available on the Freebies page of the Styer-Fitzgerald website (www.styer-fitzgerald.com). Again, you will want to have these available when potential tutors show an interest in working in your classroom.

3. Interview with you (the special education teacher) and answer application questions such as:

    - Why are you interested in becoming a peer tutor?
    - What experiences have you had that can aid you as a peer tutor?
    - If appropriate, which elective classes will you drop to become a peer tutor?

4. Visit and/or drop by and observe one of your classes before they register to begin peer tutoring.

5. Register with your school counselor to determine the type and number of credits peer tutors can receive.

> *When asked what he'd gained from his peer tutor experience, Joel said, "A bunch of great friends and life experiences I will never forget."*
>
> *Amanda said, "I became a peer tutor because I've always wanted to work in the special education field and I wanted to gain experience and joy from working with great kids."*

Training Peer Tutors

All new peer tutors should participate in an initial training session. A half-day session is recommended, but you may need to do the training over a few days rather than all on one day.

Provide ongoing training and support for students who are returning as peer tutors in order to refresh their skills. These ongoing sessions may be scheduled before school, during study periods, during lunch, or after school.

Setting Up Your Initial Training Session

During the training session, provide your new peer tutors with an agenda for the training session(s), a list of peer tutor objectives, an outline of your expectations, a description of your class and curriculum, and the grading requirements of your peer tutor program.

Provide each peer tutor with a copy of the *Peer Tutor Student Handbook* (available to purchase separately from Amazon.com, CreateSpace.com, and other retail outlets). The handbook furnishes them with information about reinforcement, correction procedures, and data collection along with specific pointers for working with individual students.

Training Agenda

Having an agenda at the beginning of the session provides your new peer tutors with information about what they can expect to learn and take away from the training. Following is a sample agenda. A downloadable copy of this agenda is available on the Freebies page of the Styer-Fitzgerald website (www.styer-fitzgerald.com). You can modify it to meet the specific needs of your training session.

Peer Tutor Training Agenda

Introduction to Peer Tutoring

- Goals and Objectives of the Training
- Disability Awareness and Etiquette
  Complete Activities #1 and #2

Teaching Methods

- **Prompts**—Initial Prompting and Fading Prompts
- **Reinforcement**—What It Is and How to Use It
  Complete Activities #3 and #4
- **Correction Procedures**—What They Are and How to Use Them
  Complete Activities #5 and #6
- **Data Collection**—Monitoring Student Progress
  Complete Activity #7

Standards and Grading

- Standards and Expectations of Peer Tutors
- Grade Requirements

Training Objectives

Following are some training objectives to share with your new peer tutors. A downloadable copy of the training objectives can be found on the Freebies page of the Styer-Fitzgerald website (www.styer-fitzgerald.com). You can modify it to meet the specific needs of your training session.

Peer Tutor Training Objectives

1. Tutors will understand what a reinforcement procedure is and how to use verbal reinforcement.

2. Tutors will learn how to use correction procedures when a student makes a mistake.

3. Tutors will be able to use data collection systems to monitor a student's progress across a variety of programs and learning activities.

4. Tutors will gain an understanding of different types of disabilities and how these disabilities affect learning.

5. Tutors will learn strategies for dealing with different students' behaviors and communication styles.

Class Description

Provide your peer tutors with a description of the curriculum and class activities you use in your classroom in the form of a handout. The following sample description is available as a downloadable file on the Freebies page of the Styer-Fitzgerald website (www.styer-fitzgerald.com). You can use it in its current format or revise it to describe your specific classroom. Remember, you are educating your peer tutors about what your special education students learn in your classroom—which typically is quite different from a peer tutor's general education.

Spend time discussing the various activities within your classroom. Encourage your peer tutors to ask questions and initiate conversations about how your special education classroom works.

The Secondary Level of The Styer-Fitzgerald Program for Functional Academics or life skills curriculum includes teaching students how to use money, tell time, write a budget, pay bills, use a computer and the phone, complete applications, fill out planners and schedules, and read sight words relating to the classroom and the community.

Students learn to use calculators, manage checking and savings accounts, and use ATM cards. In addition, special education students spend time in the community practicing these skills in grocery stores, banks, and restaurants.

This curriculum also teaches students certain vocational skills such as data entry and filing. Many of our special education students use their skills by performing jobs on campus in the counseling office, library, cafeteria, or attendance office.

Teaching Disability Awareness and Etiquette

Have your peer tutors read the section titled "Disability Awareness" in the *Peer Tutor Student Handbook* and then lead them through Activities #1 and #2.

Disability Awareness

It is important to educate your peer tutors about general disability awareness and etiquette, to help them learn how to handle difficult situations that may arise, and to teach them to work with students who are non-verbal or difficult to understand.

Interaction

Explain to your peer tutors that you set high standards and expectations for your special education students. Let them know that

- Having a disability does not give a special education student an excuse for poor behavior.

- Behaving positively and in an age-appropriate manner with your special education students is expected.

- Students in your Functional Academics or life skills program are much more *like* them than they are different from them. Therefore, they should treat each special education student as a peer.

Personal Space

Explain to your peer tutors how your special education students might inadvertently invade personal space. You might tell them that some special education students are unsure how to communicate their feelings and as a result may act inappropriately. For example, tell them that a student who likes them or wants their attention might give them a hug and not let go or grab their hands or arms without asking permission instead of simply talking to them about what's going on. Explain to the peer tutor that if a student enters his or her personal space, there are ways to respond, depending on the severity of the situation. Give your peer tutors suggestions for handling such situations. They can say things like,

- "You are in my personal space and you need to back up."

- "You didn't ask if you could hug me. You need to ask." Even if a special education student asks first, your peer tutor is not obligated to say "yes." Sometimes, it is good to say "no."

- "This is my space. That is your space. Do not enter my space."

- "You are making me uncomfortable, and you need to stop."

- "That is inappropriate. Stop, please."

Although it is rare, sometimes a special education student may become aggressive. If a student becomes agitated, suggest the following to your peer tutor:

- Tell them to say, "I can see you need a minute. I'm going to give you some space." Tell them to then move away from the student and tell you or a staff member about the situation.

- Remind them that if they cannot remember what to say, to walk away from the agitated student and immediately alert you or a staff member.

Activity #1—Helpful Responses to Inappropriate Behavior

This activity will give tutors an opportunity to practice responding to students who display inappropriate behavior. In some situations, a peer tutor might be unsure how to respond to a special education student. Let your peer tutors know this is not unusual and that it is important to learn an appropriate response for future situations. Before acting or responding, peer tutors should ask themselves, *"How will my response help this student in the future?"*

Activity #1

Have your peer tutors read the following scenario. Provide them with other real-life situations that reflect your students' individual challenges.

Jane is a sophomore with cerebral palsy and intellectual disabilities. She becomes very excited around her friends and loves to talk. She has a difficult time initiating conversation and regulating the volume of her voice. She has just asked you a question and you answered it, yet she continues asking the same question at least five more times, getting louder and louder each time.

Here are two possible ways to respond to Jane:

1. Answer her question again a couple of times then ignore her for a few times.
2. Answer her the first time only. When she asks again, tell her, "I've already answered you, Jane. I'm not going to answer again."

Explain to your peer tutors that the first response might seem like the nice thing to do, but it will not help Jane in the future. If you keep answering her and then ignoring her, she will continue to repeat the same behavior, always asking her questions over and over. Jane is a very sociable person, but no one will want to be around her if she is continuously asking the same question in a loud voice.

Explain that the second response might appear harsh. But Jane will learn that she needs to ask only once before moving on to another question or topic. The second response will help teach her. How does this response help Jane in the future? Because she is sociable, Jane MUST learn to be socially appropriate. If she learns these skills, the people around her become more accepting of her and she can experience a more fulfilled life. If she does not learn these skills, people will avoid her, and as she gets older she could become more isolated from the very society she craves.

Explain to peer tutors that sometimes the difficult reactions are those that will help students the most. Tell them that if they are unsure about how to respond to a situation, they should ask.

Communication

Discuss with your peer tutors the many ways that special education students communicate with others. Explain how communication can happen through one or more of these ways:

- Verbal
- Tactile
- Sign language
- Modified sign language

- Assistive technology (iPads, switches, computers, other devices)

- Facial expressions

- Gestures

- Utterances

- Eye gaze

- Modified "yes" or "no"

- Pictures and picture symbols

STEPS FOR COMMUNICATING

If a peer tutor does not understand a special education student, he or she should not pretend to do so. Have the peer tutor follow these steps:

1. Ask the student to repeat the communication.

2. Say, "I really want to know what you are saying. Please be patient with me and tell me again."

3. If you still do not understand, say, "I still don't understand what you just told me, so I'm going to find a staff person to help me understand."

4. Say, "Thank you for being so patient with me. I really wanted to know what you said."

RULES TO REMEMBER

In cases where peer tutors do not understand how or what special education students communicate, urge them to ask staff members to tell them. Remind peer tutors:

- That just because someone cannot speak does not mean he or she does not understand.

- Not to talk about students in front of them unless they are included in the conversation. For example, in front of a student **do not** say, "Why does he make that noise?" Instead, say, "I know you are trying to tell us something, so I am going to try to find out what it is. Does anyone know what it means when ____ makes the _____ noise?"

- That it is a very good thing to include non-verbal students in conversations about their communication. It shows that you care and that you want to understand what they are saying.

COMMUNICATING WITH NON-VERBAL STUDENTS

Help your peer tutors to understand that carrying on a conversation with someone who is non-verbal can be difficult. The special education student might not be able to respond to the peer tutor in a conventional manner. Gather resources to help your peer tutors communicate. Here are some ideas:

- Ask a staff person for items or activities the student enjoys.

- Work with families to provide photographs that your student can share with peer tutors to tell something about her/him.

- Share ideas about other topics to discuss.

- Refer to online websites and search video topics for other tips and ideas. For example, tutors can refer to the peer pages of the Washington Sensory Disabilities Services (WSDS—in Washington State) website at www.wsdsonline.org/video-library/deaf-blind-videos/peer-programs/.

- Obtain a list of suggested conversation topics and age-appropriate step-by-step social scripts to give to your peer tutors.

> **Resource Note**:
> Ideas are available, for example, on the "Can We Chat" CD by Linda Burkhart and Caroline Musselwhite. This CD is available at *www.lindaburkhart.com*.

Activity #2—Communicating Appropriately

This activity will allow your tutors to become familiar with your individual student's different communication styles.

> ### Activity #2
> It is important that your peer tutors understand the different ways in which your special education students communicate. Discuss the different types and methods of communication with your tutors, using examples of the students in your classroom.

Disability Etiquette

If you have special education students who are in wheelchairs or who have vision or hearing impairments, review the following etiquette tips with your peer tutors.

Working with Students in Wheelchairs

- When moving a person or taking a student who is in a wheelchair to another location, give a warning before moving him or her. Many special education students have heightened startle reflexes and might be easily upset without first knowing what to expect. Follow these steps:

  1. Tap the student on the shoulder and move to a place where he or she can see and hear you.

  2. Begin with the student's name and say, "____, we are going to go to _____ now, and I'm going to push you there."

  3. Say, "Are you ready?" or "Here we go."

- If a student is not in his or her wheelchair and you need to move the chair, let the student know what you intend to do and where you will move it.

- **Never** hold onto or sit in a student's empty wheelchair—the wheelchair is part of the student's personal space.

Working with Hearing-Impaired, Visually-Impaired, or Deaf-Blind Students

- If you have a student who is deaf and has an interpreter, be sure to talk to the student and not to the interpreter.

- If you have a student who is blind, talk about what is going on around him or her. For example, "Did you hear the door close? Sally Smith just came into the classroom; she's hanging up her coat."

- As you approach someone who has a dual sensory impairment (deaf-blindness), begin by tapping the person on the shoulder. Then move your hand down the students arm until you reach his or her hand; then give your identifier (go to www.pathstoliteracy.org/blog/using-personal-identifiers-my-deafblind-son/ for more information). Remember that some students with deaf-blindness often have some hearing and vision. If that is the case, identify yourself verbally or show them your picture so they know who you are.

- When working with students who are deaf-blind, be sure to put your hands underneath their hands rather than grabbing the tops of their hands and manipulating them. This is called "hand-under-hand."

- When you walk with a student who is blind or deaf-blind, offer him/her your arm. Watch for and warn about changes in the terrain, transition strips, doorways, etc. At all times you must be aware of your surroundings so that you can give the student appropriate directions for navigating the environment. **It is recommended that if a peer tutor is going to work with a student who is blind or deaf-blind that they receive training by an expert such as the district TVI first.**

Teaching Methodology

Helping your peer tutors to understand the methodology of working with special education students is essential to the tutors' success in your classroom. You will need to train them in the use of prompts and how to apply reinforcement techniques and correction procedures.

Teaching Prompts

A vital part of your peer tutor program is ensuring that your tutors understand what prompts are and how to use them. Teach tutors that a prompt is a cue that tells students what it is you are asking them to do. In the community setting, the prompt or cue can be the sign at the crosswalk that flashes "Don't Walk." In the classroom during a teaching session, the prompt or cue is the teacher or peer tutor giving an instruction—for example, "Give me $4.99," or "What time is it?"

It is important for peer tutors to understand how to use prompts, whether working with students in the classroom or out in the community. They also need to know how to determine when prompts are no longer needed and should be faded. Peer tutors should review the "Prompting" section in their student handbooks as you teach them about prompts. Use Activity #6, Prompting, Reinforcement, and Correction Procedures Practice, to practice prompts. Be sure to emphasize the following points.

Prompts during Direct Instruction

When teaching a skill in the classroom (direct instruction):

- Make the prompts clear. Tell special education students exactly what you want them to do. For example, "Give me $4.99."

- Vary the prompts so that students learn that a variety of cues have the same meaning (for example, you can say "$4.99" or "That will be $4.99.")

Prompts in the Real Environment

When teaching a skill in the community (real environment), you will use prompts or cues that occur naturally in that environment. For example, at a street corner, rather than using a verbal prompt of "Stop," point to the "Walk/Don't Walk" sign and say, "That sign says *Walk*; that means go." Or say, "That sign says *Don't Walk*; that means stop or wait."

Fading Prompts

When peer tutors are teaching a skill initially, their prompts should be frequent and concise. After a student begins to learn a skill in the real environment, the peer tutor should give him the chance to respond on his own before prompting for a response. As students learn a skill, the need for prompts decreases, thus, they can use prompts less frequently—"fading" them.

Peer Tutors know they have successfully taught a skill when:

- The student responds to natural cues in the community/environment, such as "Walk/Don't Walk" signs.

- The student responds correctly to prompts in the classroom, regardless of how they are presented (for example, whether you say, "$4.99," "Give me $4.99," or "$4.99 please," the response is correct).

More information about prompting can be found in *The Styer-Fitzgerald Program for Functional Academics.*

Teaching Reinforcement and Correction Procedures

Provide your peer tutors with basic "how to" instructions so that they gain skill in working with special education students and have a positive experience in your classroom.

As you train tutors, introduce reinforcement and correction procedures simultaneously. Presenting these concepts together is important because both procedures are necessary in order for special education students to learn new skills. Your students learn new skills or behaviors when their responses are immediately followed with reinforcement (usually verbal) for correct responses, or correction procedures for incorrect responses. Because reinforcement and correction procedures are equally important teaching tools, it is essential that your peer tutors understand how to use them.

With the exception of the Activities, the following sections on reinforcement and correction procedures are also presented in the *Peer Tutor Student Handbook.* Have your peer tutors refer to the "Reinforcement and Correction Procedures" section in their handbooks. Then do Activities #3, #4, and #5 as shown in the following sections.

Reinforcement

By reinforcing a correct response or behavior, peer tutors increase the likelihood of the reoccurrence of that behavior. In other words:

BEHAVIOR > SOMETHING "GOOD" HAPPENS > BEHAVIOR IS LIKELY TO RECUR
          (*Reinforcement*)

TYPES OF REINFORCEMENT

It is important that your peer tutors understand that there are different types of reinforcement. They also need to know which method is appropriate and when to use it. Discuss the three types of reinforcement: verbal, physical, and tangible.

Verbal Reinforcement

Verbal reinforcement consists of praise or other words of encouragement. For example, "I like how you are staying on task." Or "You really are working hard!"

Physical Reinforcement

There are different types of physical reinforcement, and each needs to be age-appropriate. For example, a hug might be appropriate for an elementary-aged student whereas a pat on the back or a "high five" is more natural and acceptable when working with a secondary-aged student.

Tangible Reinforcement

Items that a student can touch or that have value to a special education student can provide tangible reinforcement. Examples of tangible reinforcement can include items such as a paycheck, a token, a '+' on a card, or a certificate of work well done.

DETERMINING THE TYPE OF REINFORCEMENT TO USE

Help your peer tutors to understand that the needs of an individual student or the particular lesson being taught often determine the type of reinforcement that will be appropriate. The type of reinforcement is also often a matter of preference of an individual special education student; what works with one student may or may not be effective with another.

You can combine different types of reinforcement. For example, saying "Nice work," while giving a "high five" combines verbal with physical reinforcement.

FREQUENCY OF REINFORCEMENT

The frequency of reinforcement depends on where the student is in his or her learning process. Explain to peer tutors when to use continuous versus intermittent reinforcement.

Continuous Reinforcement

Deliver this method of reinforcement after each and every correct response. Continuous reinforcement is generally used when a student is initially learning a skill.

Intermittent Reinforcement

Deliver this method of reinforcement after a random number of correct responses. Applying intermittent reinforcement is generally used for a student who has learned a skill but still requires feedback about the accuracy of his or her performance.

DELIVERING REINFORCEMENT

Peer tutors need to understand that it is vital to the learning process that reinforcement be delivered:

- Immediately
- Clearly
- Frequently

Activities #3 and #4—Reinforcement

These two activities will be helpful for generating ideas about possible reinforcement phrases.

Activity #3

Have peer tutors brainstorm about reinforcement examples that they have found successful. If tutors are familiar with your special education students, ask them to name some of the responses that are reinforcing for those students.

Activity #4

Ask peer tutors to think of different ways to say "good job" (refer to "Pointers for Giving Praise" in Appendix B).

Note: Another helpful strategy is to post examples of verbal reinforcement in your classroom so that tutors, as well as paraeducators and other personnel, have access to these ideas while they are working with your students.

Correction Procedures

Using correction procedures appropriately can help increase the skill levels of special education students as effectively as positive reinforcement does. It is important for peer tutors to understand how to use correction procedures so that special education students will learn from their mistakes.

Remind peer tutors to use correction procedures that are educational rather than injurious to a student's self-esteem. Give your peer tutors the following tips:

- Be positive. Avoid saying, "No, that's not right."

- Use steps like these in the following example:

    1. When there is a mistake, say, "Stop" or "Wait," so that the mistake does not continue and become ingrained.

    2. Then say, "Watch me." (Model the behavior, such as: "This is $1.20" and count out the amount.)

    3. Say, "Now you try."

    4. Then reinforce a correct response, such as: "That's right; that is $1.20."

Activity #5—Correction Procedures

This activity will give tutors the opportunity to practice responding to both correct and incorrect responses.

Activity #5

Have peer tutors role-play a one-to-one teaching session and practice both reinforcing correct responses and using correction procedures for incorrect responses.

Begin by having a tutor play the role of one of the special education students in your class with you in the role as teacher, modeling both reinforcement and correction procedures.

After demonstrating the teacher-student interaction, have your tutors practice the role of the teacher.

Summary of Reinforcement and Correction Procedures with Lesson Samples

Remind peer tutors that:

- When they use reinforcement and correction procedures, both need to be immediate and clear.

- When reinforcing, it is the response or behavior that just occurred that will be strengthened, especially if it is followed up with verbal praise (reinforcement).

- Clear and **specific** praise helps a student understand exactly what he or she did correctly. For instance, saying "nice job" lets the student know that he did the right thing, but it does not tell the student what the right thing was. It is better to be specific and say, for example, "Nice job counting out $4.99."

- It might be difficult for peer tutors to correct special education students because they do not want to hurt anyone's feelings. But assure tutors that when they use correction procedures appropriately, the students they work with are learning. The experience becomes educational rather than ego-deflating.

REINFORCEMENT SAMPLE

The following sample is taken from lessons presented in *The Styer-Fitzgerald Program for Functional Academics* Curriculum. Note the reinforcement for the correct response.

Prompt	Correct Response	Reinforcement
Say, "Give me $4.99."	Student counts out five one-dollar bills.	Say, "Nice job giving me $4.99."

CORRECTION PROCEDURE SAMPLE

The following sample is taken from lessons in *The Styer- Fitzgerald Program for Functional Academics* Curriculum. Note the correction procedure for the incorrect response.

Prompt	Response	Correction Procedure
Say, "Give me $4.99."	Student counts, "One, two, four."	When the student makes the mistake, immediately say, "Stop." Repeat the prompt: "$4.99." Say, "Watch me; one, two, three, four, ninety-nine. Now it's your turn."

The example shows how the teacher stops the student immediately when the mistake was made or when the number three was skipped. Therefore, the student does not learn that four follows two in the sequence. If you do not stop the student at the point of the mistake and he or she keeps counting, the sequence is learned as "one, two, four…" rather than "one, two, three, four…"

After stopping the student, you must clearly demonstrate the correct response. In other words, "Watch me. This is $4.99" as you count out "one, two, three, four…"

It is natural to want to just say "no," and give the student the correct answer, and then move on to the next trial. However, doing this does not provide the student with the information needed to learn the skill you are trying to teach.

Activity #6—Prompting, Reinforcement, and Correction Procedures Practice

This activity will give the tutor the opportunity to combine all phases of instruction: prompting and using reinforcement or a correction procedure.

Activity #6

Have your peer tutors role-play teaching a skill such as telling time by quarter hours as in this sample from *The Styer-Fitzgerald Program for Functional Academics* Curriculum.

Prompt	Correct Response	Correction Procedure	Data
Verbal students: Present the student with the clock and ask, "What time is it?" **Non-verbal students:** Use three cards rather than an analog clock. Say, "Show me _____ (e.g., *9:30*)."	**Verbal students:** Student says the correct time (e.g., *9:30*). **Non-verbal students:** Student points to the correct card.	Say, "No. It is _____ (e.g., *9:30*)." Repeat the prompt (with the same time, e.g., *9:30*) and ask "What time is it?" (verbal) Or "Show me _____." (non-verbal) Reinforce the correct response.	**Correct Response:** Circle the corresponding number on the data sheet. **Incorrect Response:** Put a slash through the corresponding number.

Begin by having your tutors play the role of the special education student as you model prompting, reinforcement, and correction procedures. Next, change roles and have tutors practice their teaching skills.

Teaching Data Collection

Data is used to evaluate a student's present level of performance—called "baseline data." Additional data is collected to track student progress and to determine when to move on to the next level of the skill or program.

Data is also used to analyze whether you need to make changes to individual student programs. For example, if a student has made little or no progress, it might be time to try a new skill or break the skill into easier segments.

This Peer Tutoring program references the two primary types of data collection as described in *The Styer-Fitzgerald Program for Functional Academics*. If you are using the Functional Academics program in your classroom, it is recommended that you review the "Data Recording" section in the Curriculum. The two methods of data collection most used are:

- Discrete Trial format
- Task Analysis format

The following sections define these format types and show a sample of each type of data sheet.

Discrete Trial—Recording the Percentage Correct

In the discrete trial data system, the peer tutor records correct responses with circles and incorrect responses with slashes. They are then able to summarize the data by calculating the daily percentage correct for each lesson.

Peer tutors should run a minimum of ten trials per day and record data accordingly.

The discrete trial data sheet is the type peer tutors will use when teaching skills such as time-telling or counting coins. Here is an example of a discrete trial data sheet with sample data and the percentage correct highlighted by the square.

Date:	9/1	9/2	9/3											Correct
	10	10	10	10	10	10	10	10	10	10	10	10	10	100%
	9	9	9	9	9	9	9	9	9	9	9	9	9	90%
	8	8	8	8	8	8	8	8	8	8	8	8	8	80%
	7	7	7	7	7	7	7	7	7	7	7	7	7	70%
	6	6	6	6	6	6	6	6	6	6	6	6	6	60%
	5	5	5	5	5	5	5	5	5	5	5	5	5	50%
	4	4	4	4	4	4	4	4	4	4	4	4	4	40%
	3	3	3	3	3	3	3	3	3	3	3	3	3	30%
	2	2	2	2	2	2	2	2	2	2	2	2	2	20%
	1	1	1	1	1	1	1	1	1	1	1	1	1	10%

Prompt: "Give me _____."

Task Analysis—Recording the Number of Prompts

The task analysis format generally counts the number of prompts per step that are required for a student to perform a particular task or skill. Peer tutors teach the skill and record the number of prompts per step until the student can perform the entire task independently.

If a student has difficulty with a particular step, you will need to break the task into smaller/simpler steps until the student can perform the task independently.

A task analysis is the format of the data sheet peer tutors will use when they teach skills in the community, such as street crossing and grocery shopping. Here is an example of a task analysis sheet with sample data.

Task Analysis		Initials: AB	Initials: AB	Initials:	Initials:	Initials:
		Date: 9/1	Date: 9/4	Date:	Date:	Date:
		Prompts	Prompts	Prompts	Prompts	Prompts
1	Finds nearest bus stop	//	/			
2	Finds bus number	/	/			
3	Gets on correct bus	//	//			
4	Pays/shows pass	/	/			
5	Finds a seat	//	/			
6	Pulls cord prior to stop	/	/			
7	Exits the bus	/	/			
	Total Number of Prompts	10	8			
	Bus Stop Location	3rd & Main	B Street			
	Final Destination	17th St.	J Street			

Accuracy in Data Collection

It is not uncommon for peer tutors to misunderstand what constitutes a prompt and to mark data sheets incorrectly. Be sure to monitor your tutors, helping them to understand and account for the correct number of trials and types of prompts when using both the task analysis form and the discrete trial format.

It is important for peer tutors to understand that they are not being mean when they are marking responses as incorrect. The rule is: if reinforcing the student, the response is marked as correct. However, if the peer tutor was required to do a correction procedure, the response is marked as incorrect even if the student goes on to respond accurately after having been corrected.

The following diagram illustrates the rule of when to record a response as correct or incorrect.

Prompt ➡ Correct Response ➡ Reinforcement (draw a circle on discrete trial data sheet)

Prompt ➡ Incorrect Response ➡ Correction Procedure (draw a slash on discrete trial data sheet and a hash mark on task analysis data sheets)

Have tutors initial the days/dates that they collect data. This helps if you need to investigate and account for unusual data on a particular date. It is a good idea to have your tutors note on the data sheets any dates that a special education student might have been affected by illness, lack of sleep, and classroom interruptions.

Activity #7—Practice Gathering Data

This activity allows tutors to practice taking data that indicates both correct and incorrect responses.

Activity #7

Have peer tutors role-play a couple of lessons using both types of data sheets. Have one tutor take data while you and another tutor role-play instruction. Be sure tutors have a chance to collect both types of data. Check their work and make constructive comments to ensure their accuracy.

Go to the Freebies page of the Styer-Fitzgerald website (www.styer-fitzgerald.com) to download blank data sheets for this activity.

Involving Your Peer Tutors in Multiple Ways

Before peer tutors begin working with your special education students, have them observe you, a paraeducator, or a seasoned peer tutor as they work with students. After a new peer tutor is comfortable with the lesson he or she has observed, have him or her perform the task with the student. Do not require new peer tutors to record data until they are comfortable with prompting, reinforcement, and correction procedures. Periodically observe individual tutors to be sure their data collection skills are reliable.

There are many activities in which your peer tutors can participate, help teach, and model appropriate behavior for your special education students. Activities include, but are not limited to things such as:

- Lunch time—have peer tutors "hang out" with a special education buddy during the lunch hour.

- Pep assemblies—have your peer tutors sit with your students and model appropriate school spirit in that setting.

- Field trips or community outings—include your peer tutors for age-appropriate modeling.

Peer Tutors Serve as Examples

Be sure your peer tutors understand that they will become important examples to the students in your special education classroom. Peer tutors can foster healthy relationships by:

- Modeling appropriate behavior.

- Assisting students in their general education classrooms, when appropriate.

- Practicing greetings and simple communication and social skills with your special education students.

- Working with students at school job sites, for example as an office assistant, on lunchroom duty, during classroom cleanup, at the student store, or helping to count money at fundraisers.

Foster opportunities for peer tutors to converse with your special education students, modeling behavior using symbols and augmentative communication devices.

Have a tutor become the "voice" for a student who uses a voice output device by programming his or her voice into the device. Choose two or three peer tutors to record then select the voice for which the special education student has an affinity or preference. Have the selected peer tutor then program all voice output devices for that student. For voice output, it is appropriate to pair your tutors with students of the same age and gender.

Peer Tutors Can Use Their Strengths

Look for each tutor's individual strengths and match those strengths to the tasks, programs, and students' needs in your special education classroom. For example, if you have an extroverted peer tutor who enjoys telling stories, have that tutor entertain or keep company with a special education student during physical therapy time. This can provide a useful distraction for special education students who experience pain during physical therapy.

Setting Standards and Grading Peer Tutors

Set standards that peer tutors must meet in order to be successful and earn a particular grade. Tutors should think about their role in the classroom as a job, a task that requires them to be responsible and reliable.

Expectations of Your Peer Tutors

Following are some suggested expectations. Be sure to discuss them with your students during the training session. Add to this list any other expectations you want to share with your tutors. Have your peer tutors take notes, ask questions, and bring up any questions about these expectations.

Attendance

Be sure peer tutor attendance in your classroom is required on scheduled days and times. Students should maintain timesheets. Absences are treated as in other classes (i.e., excused, unexcused, or tardy).

Attitude

Expect your peer tutor to have a positive attitude and to act in an age-appropriate manner with students in the special education classroom. Disrespectful or negative behavior should not be tolerated.

Training

Have peer tutors participate in a minimum of three hours (approximately a half day) of training at the beginning of each term. These sessions may be scheduled before school, during study periods, during lunch, or after school. You might want to waive training during subsequent terms for students who enroll as peer tutors for more than one term.

Teaching

Expect peer tutors to assist with teaching students in the Functional Academics or life skills program to learn social, leisure, vocational, and academic skills.

Data Collection

Teach peer tutors to correctly collect data and record a student's progress in each of the individualized programs.

Weekly Meetings

Meet weekly with peer tutors. Meetings should be scheduled at a time convenient to both the teacher and the tutor and last approximately twenty minutes. During these meetings peer tutors should receive feedback about their students' programs, classroom issues, and peer tutor performance. Schedule these meetings less frequently or for shorter time if you find you communicate frequently on an informal basis with your peer tutors.

Peer Tutor Questions

Allow students to ask questions, making it clear to them that no question is offensive or silly if asked appropriately. Instruct peer tutors to ask questions that are specific to particular special education students in privacy. Let them know they should come to you or another staff person rather than asking the question in front of other students.

Grading

There are basic tasks or activities that tutors should perform regularly in order to earn their peer tutoring grades:

- Spend time (2-3 activities) with special education students outside of regular peer tutor classroom time. This can be on campus but not during regularly scheduled class. Some examples are assemblies, break times, and lunch periods.

- Keep a journal of classroom experiences working with students with disabilities. Blank journal pages are provided in the back of each *Peer Tutor Student Handbook*. (If you, the teacher, prefer to have the students keep these journals online and submit them to you that way, indicate that during the initial peer tutor training session.)

- Educate other general education students (the peers of the peer tutors) about disabilities.

For most special education students, social life is limited or even nonexistent. They often do not have circles of friends that mirror the types of relationships common to their typically developing peers. Therefore, requiring peer tutors to engage with your special education students in situations outside the classroom can facilitate friendships that might not happen without some guidance and support.

While the grade requirements track the number of times tutors are required to spend time with a student outside of class, peer tutors will often exceed the requirement. To monitor the number and quality of interactions, ask peer tutors to document what they did and with whom. The form, Social Interactions Outside of the Class Setting, is available on the Freebies page of the Styer-Fitzgerald website (www.styer-fitzgerald.com). You can download it, modify it, and print to give to your peer tutors.

Grade Requirements

The following grade requirements are suggestions and appear in the *Peer Tutor Student Handbook*. A downloadable file is provided on the Freebies page of the Styer-Fitzgerald website (www.styer-fitzgerald.com). You can modify the form to meet your specific requirements.

If you modify the "Grade Requirements" form, hand it out to your peer tutors and have them clip or staple the form inside their student handbooks. Have your tutors review the requirements and write the due dates in their handbooks.

To Maintain an "A"

- Spend time with a special education student, three times per term, outside of class time.

- Keep a weekly record using "My Peer Tutor Journal" found in the back of the student handbook. Write about experiences as a peer tutor working with special education students. Turn in the journal at least three times per semester. The first due date is _____.

- Educate at least one peer about disabilities. Explain to the special education teacher how you accomplished this.

To Maintain a "B"

- Spend time with a special education student, two times per term, outside of class time.

- Keep a weekly record using "My Peer Tutor Journal" found in the back of the student handbook. Write about experiences as a peer tutor working with special education students. Turn in the journal at least three times per semester. The first due date is _____.

- Educate at least one peer about disabilities. Explain to the special education teacher how you accomplished this.

To Maintain a "C"

- Work with special education students in class.

- Keep a weekly record using "My Peer Tutor Journal" found in the back of the student handbook. Write about experiences as a peer tutor working with special education students. Turn in the journal at least three times per semester. The first due date is_____.

- Educate at least one of your peers about disabilities. Explain to the special education teacher how you accomplished this.

Ongoing Success of Your Tutors and Your Program

Be sure always to explain why you do what you do and why you are asking the peer tutor to perform a specific activity. For example, explain why it is better to use the practice of hand-under-hand rather than hand-over-hand prompting, or tell why a special education student with dual sensory impairment needs more time to process information. As you provide explanations, your peer tutors will be learning the reasoning behind your teaching methods. This will also help them more easily understand why incorporating certain strategies can enhance the progress of a special education student. Your clear explanations may thus also remove any concerns a peer tutor might have about procedures that seem unhelpful or unnecessary.

Here are additional recommendations to help you ensure that your peer tutors both enjoy and benefit from working in your classroom.

- Maintain an organized classroom so peer tutors feel connected and needed.

- Provide peer tutors with "To Do" lists so they can accomplish tasks, activities, or errands during down time or when one of their students is absent. See the sample "To Do Checklist" on the Freebies page of the Styer-Fitzgerald website (www.styer-fitzgerald.com).

- Implement an open-door policy, encouraging your peer tutors to stop by during their non-class hours. Encourage them to bring their friends.

- Check in with your peer tutors regularly to find out if they have questions or concerns they may not have raised during their time with students. It is a good idea to hold "staff meetings" with your peer tutors on a monthly basis to provide an opportunity for tutors to raise issues or brainstorm solutions for difficulties they might have with particular students.

- Provide recognition of the accomplishments of your peer tutors. Let your tutors know you appreciate their contribution to your classroom and especially to the academic and social growth of your special education students. You can recognize your peer tutors by writing them personal thank-you notes or by creating award certificates and presenting them at a school assembly. There are samples of thank-you letters on the Freebies page of the Styer-Fitzgerald website (www.styer-fitzgerald.com). You can personalize these for your tutors.

> *Bringing students with disabilities together with their peers who do not have disabilities is a win-win situation for everyone involved.*

The Styer-Fitzgerald
Program for Functional
Academics

Appendix A—Helpful Forms

These forms are available for your convenience as Microsoft Word® documents on the Freebies page of the Styer-Fitzgerald website (www.styer-fitzgerald.com). You can download the files, edit them to meet your specific needs, and print them for use in your peer tutoring program.

Permission to Talk About Specific Students and Disabilities

I am asking for permission to discuss your child's disability with his or her peers at school. Over the years, I have had several students ask me specifically about students in my class and about their particular disabilities. Understanding is the key to encouraging acceptance; however, I am not comfortable sharing information about your child without your permission.

Be assured that I will respect whatever your comfort level is with disclosing personal information. I will use my discretion during our discussions, but I would like to know your specific feelings or concerns on the matter and what you are comfortable having me share. When peers are able to inquire openly about disabilities, they then appreciate and understand our students and their very unique abilities.

If, for any reason, you are uncomfortable with having me share information, please do not hesitate to let me know. Also, if you have literature or website recommendations with information about your child's disability that you think his or her peers would appreciate, please send those to me at your convenience.

Thank you for your time.

Sincerely,

_____

I give you permission to discuss my child's specific disability with his or her peers for educational purposes. I understand that I can withdraw my permission at any time. This permission form is valid until I request otherwise.

_____   _____
Parent Signature   Date

Specific Information you would like me to share:

_____
_____
_____
_____
_____

General topics or information you would prefer I avoid sharing:

_____
_____
_____
_____
_____

Peer Tutor Application

Date: _____

Name: _____Grade: _____

List two references of people who know you well, such as teachers, friends, counselors, etc.

Name of Reference   Phone Number   Relationship to You

1. _____

2. _____

Briefly tell why you are interested in becoming a peer tutor and working with a life skills/functional academics program.

_____

_____

_____

Briefly describe any experience(s) you have had that might be helpful to you in a position as a peer tutor in a life skills/functional academics program.

_____

_____

_____

Which of your current elective classes would you prefer to drop in order to be a peer tutor?

_____

_____

Please present a Peer Tutor Reference form to each of two teachers who know you well.

These may be current teachers or teachers you have had in the past.

_____   _____

Student Signature   Date   Parent Signature   Date

Peer Tutor: Teacher Reference Form

Date: _____

Student Name: _____ Grade: _____

The student named above is interested in working in the Life Skills/Functional Academics classroom as a peer tutor. Please complete this questionnaire and return it to _____ as soon as possible. Thank you.

Teacher's Name: _____

How long have you known this student? _____

Based on your experience with this student, please rate him or her in the following areas:

Dependability:	Excellent	Fair	Needs Work
Quality of work:	Excellent	Fair	Needs Work
Empathy:	Excellent	Fair	Needs Work
Follow-through:	Excellent	Fair	Needs Work

Comments:

_____

_____

_____

In your opinion, how will this student function in the role of a peer tutor to students with disabilities?

_____

_____

Do you have any concerns about this student working with students who have disabilities? What are your concerns?

_____

_____

_____

Appendix B—Pointers for Giving Praise

When you praise one of your special education students, be specific and encourage the response or behavior you want to see again. Here are some suggestions:

"Nice job...

paying attention."

following directions."

listening to instructions."

acting like an adult."

speaking like an adult."

staying on task."

working hard."

"I like how you...

are in your own space."

are sitting like an adult."

have your hands and feet to yourself."

are following directions."

are listening to directions."

are trying hard."

are acting like a high school student."

are *now* using a quieter tone of voice."

Some Other Words of Praise

"You're doing a much better job working."

"That's the way to act like an adult."

"Thank you for working quietly."

"I'm so glad you made the right choice."

Notes

Notes

Notes

About the Authors

Together, Candice and Suzanne have over 40 years of teaching experience in special education and have developed peer tutor programs in every classroom they've worked in. Their peer tutoring model of reverse inclusion maximizes peer interaction in natural and appropriate ways. They were inspired to share their experiences recruiting and training peer tutors knowing the positive effects that these programs have on both special education students and the general education students who work as peer tutors.

Dr. Candice Styer has worked in the field of special education for over 30 years. She received her teaching certification, M.Ed., and Ph.D. at the University of Oregon. She developed the life skills assessment and curriculum over the last 30 years while teaching middle school and high school students with moderate and severe disabilities.

Suzanne Fitzgerald has worked with children and adults with developmental, physical, emotional, and behavioral disabilities in classroom, vocational, residential, and recreational settings for the past 21 years. She received her Bachelor of Arts degree in Human Services from Western Washington University and her Teaching Certification and Masters in Special Education degree from the University of Washington. Suzanne was a middle and high school special education teacher for the Snohomish School District.

Additional Curriculum by Dr. Candice Styer and Suzanne Fitzgerald

The Styer-Fitzgerald Program for Functional Academics

A unique approach to teaching functional skills to students with mild, moderate, and severe disabilities, including autism. The comprehensive assessment and curriculum teach independent skills that focus on each student's individual needs. Teachers themselves, Candice and Suzanne developed and tested the program in classrooms serving students with a variety of disabilities.

Elementary Level

- 11 Academic and Life Skills Units
- Teaching Guide with Implementation Tools
- Program Masters (includes Lesson Plans and Data Sheets)
- Portfolio Teacher's Manual
- Over 200 pages in reproducibles, including Teaching Materials, Progress-Tracking Data Sheets, Curriculum Progress Guide, Present Levels of Performance Chart, Student Portfolio Forms
- Assessment Teacher's Manual
- Assessment Testing Kit
- Teaching Materials Kit (included in Deluxe Teaching Package)

Secondary Level

- 10 Academic and Life Skills Units
- Teaching Guide with Implementation Tools
- Program Masters (includes Lesson Plans and Data Sheets)
- Portfolio Teacher's Manual
- Over 100 pages of reproducibles, including Teaching Materials, Progress-Tracking Data Sheets, Curriculum Progress Guide, Present Levels of Performance Chart, Student Portfolio Forms
- Assessment Teacher's Manual
- Assessment Testing Kit
- Teaching Materials Kit (included in Deluxe Teaching Package)

Additional Titles:

Life after School: Transition Planning for Students with Disabilities

Titles Available on Amazon.com, CreateSpace.com, and other retail outlets:

Effective Strategies for Working with Paraeducators
Paraeducator Handbook

Teacher's Guide to Peer Tutoring
Peer Tutor Handbook

For more information, please visit the Styer-Fitzgerald website at **www.SDESworks.com**.

The Styer-Fitzgerald
Program for Functional Academics

Peer Tutor

Secondary Level

Student Handbook
(Teacher's Copy)

Created by

CANDICE STYER, Ph.D.

AND

SUZANNE FITZGERALD, M.Ed.

Published by

Specially Designed
Education Services

The Styer-Fitzgerald Program for Functional Academics
Peer Tutor Student Handbook

First U.S. Edition Published in 2015

SPECIALLY DESIGNED EDUCATION SERVICES
18223 102ND AVE NE
SUITE B
BOTHELL, WA 98011

www.SDESworks.com

ISBN 978-0-9969130-5-8

Cover Design by

hewitt
by design

www.hewittbydesign.com

A big thank you to our editor extraordinaire, Debbie Austin.

Used by permission from The Styer-Fitzgerald Program for Functional Academics, Secondary Level
©2013 Candice Styer and Suzanne Fitzgerald, Lesson Plans and Data Sheets

Printed by CreateSpace, An Amazon.com Company

CONTENTS

Welcome, Peer Tutor!

Congratulations! You have been accepted as a peer tutor in the Functional Academics / life skills program. As a peer tutor, you will make a positive difference in the lives of your peers with disabilities.

Expectations of Peer Tutors

As a peer tutor, you are responsible for your own regular attendance, positive attitude, ongoing training, teaching, monitoring student progress, and attending weekly meetings. Here are some details.

Regular Attendance

You will maintain a timesheet to show attendance. Absences are treated as in other classes (i.e., excused, unexcused, or tardy).

Positive Attitude

As a peer tutor, you are expected to have a positive attitude and to act in an age-appropriate manner with students in the special education classroom. Disrespectful or negative behavior is not tolerated.

Ongoing Training

You are expected to participate in a minimum of ___ hours of training at the beginning of each term. These sessions may be scheduled before school, during study periods, during lunch, or after school. Check with the special education teacher.

Teaching

As a peer tutor you will assist with teaching the students in the Functional Academics or life skills program as they learn social, leisure, vocational, and academic skills.

Monitoring Student Progress

It is important for you to learn to correctly collect data and to record each student's progress as you help with individualized programs.

Ask Questions

- Always ask questions! No question is offensive or silly if asked appropriately.

- If a question is specific to a particular student, be sure to ask the teacher or another staff person privately and not in front of other students.

Weekly Meetings

You should plan to meet weekly with the special education teacher. Meetings, lasting about 20 minutes, will be scheduled at a time convenient to both you and the special education teacher. During these meetings you will receive feedback about your students' programs, classroom issues, and your performance as a peer tutor.

Notes

Disability Awareness and Etiquette

Teachers set high standards and expectations for their special education students and the peer tutors who help teach. Here are some things to remember during your service as a peer tutor.

Disability Awareness

It is important to be aware of your peers with disabilities and to learn to interact with them, handling situations with consideration and care.

Interaction

Here are some important things to keep in mind as you interact with special education students.

- Having a disability does not give a special education student an excuse for poor behavior.
- Peer tutors are expected to behave positively and in an age-appropriate manner as they interact with special education students.
- Special education students in the Functional Academics or life skills program are much more like you than they are different. Therefore, as a peer tutor, you should treat each special education student as a peer.

Personal Space

Special education students might inadvertently invade your personal space. Remember that some special education students are unsure how to communicate their feelings and as a result might act inappropriately. For example, a student who likes you or wants your attention might give you a hug and not let go, or grab your hand or arm without asking permission instead of simply talking to you about his or her feelings.

A special education student may also say something that is inappropriate or makes you uncomfortable such as "You are pretty and I love you." It is alright to confront the student and let them know that talking to friends like this is not okay. You could say "I like you, too, but telling people outside of your family that you love them is not okay and it makes people uncomfortable."

If a student enters your personal space, there are ways to respond, depending on the severity of the situation. The following are suggestions for things to say when handling such situations.

- "You are in my personal space and you need to back up."
- "You didn't ask if you could hug me. You need to ask." Even if a special education student asks first, you are not obligated to say "yes." Sometimes, It Is good to say "no."
- "This is my space. That is your space. Do not enter my space."
- "You are making me uncomfortable and you need to stop."
- "That is inappropriate. Stop, please."

Although it is rare, sometimes a special education student can become aggressive. If a student becomes agitated, remember the following:

- Say, "I can see you need a minute. I'm going to give you some space." Immediately move away from the student and tell the teacher or a staff member about the situation.

- If you cannot remember what to say, walk away from the student and immediately alert a teacher or staff member.

Helpful Responses

There might be times or situations when you are unsure about how to respond to a special education student. This is not unusual. However, it is important to learn an appropriate response for these possible situations. Before acting or responding, you should ask yourself:

"How will my response help this student in the future?"

How to Communicate

There are many ways that special education students communicate with others, including their peer tutors. Communication can happen through one or more of these ways:

- Verbal

- Tactile

- Sign language

- Modified sign language

- Assistive technology (iPads, switches, computers)

- Facial expressions

- Gestures

- Utterances

- Eye gaze

- Modified "yes" or "no"

- Pictures and picture symbols

STEPS FOR COMMUNICATING

If you do not understand a special education student, do not pretend to do so. Follow these steps:

1. Ask the student to repeat the communication.

2. Say, "I really want to know what you are saying. Please be patient with me and tell me again."

3. If you still do not understand, say, "I still don't understand what you just told me, so I'm going to find a staff person to help me understand."

4. Say, "Thank you for being so patient with me. I really wanted to know what you said."

RULES TO REMEMBER

In cases where you do not understand how or what a special education student is trying to communicate, ask a staff member to tell you. Remember:

- Just because someone cannot speak does not mean he or she does not understand.

- Do not talk about students in front of them unless they are included in the conversation. For example, in front of a student **do not** say, "Why does he make that noise?" Instead, say, "I know you are trying to tell us something, so I am going to try to find out what it is. Does anyone know what it means when _____ makes the _____ noise?"

- It is a very good thing to include non-verbal students in conversations about their communication. It shows that you care and that you want to understand what they are saying.

COMMUNICATING WITH NON-VERBAL STUDENTS

Carrying on a conversation with someone who is non-verbal can be difficult. The special education student might not be able to respond to you in a conventional manner. Here are suggestions:

- Ask a staff person for items or activities the student enjoys.

- Ask the student if there are pictures he or she can share that tell about him or her.

- Ask the teacher for ideas about other topics to talk about.

- Refer to online websites and search video topics for other tips and ideas. For example, you can refer to the peer pages on the Washington Sensory Disabilities Services (WSDS—in Washington State) website at www.wsdsonline.org/video-library/deaf-blind-videos/peer-programs/.

- If it is available in your classroom, ask your teacher for a list of suggested conversational topics and age-appropriate step-by-step social scripts.

Disability Etiquette

WORKING WITH STUDENTS IN WHEELCHAIRS

- To take a student who is in a wheelchair to another location, give a warning before moving him or her. Many special education students have heightened startle reflexes and might be easily upset without first knowing what to expect. Follow these steps:

  1. Tap the student on the shoulder and move to a place where he or she can see and hear you.

  2. Begin with the student's name and say, "_____, we are going to go to _____ now, and I'm going to push you there."

  3. Say, "Are you ready?" or "Here we go."

- If a student is not in his or her wheelchair and you need to move the chair, let the student know what you intend to do and where you will move it.

- **NEVER** hold onto or sit in a student's empty wheelchair—the wheelchair is part of the student's personal space.

WORKING WITH HEARING-IMPAIRED, VISUALLY-IMPAIRED, OR DEAF-BLIND STUDENTS

- If you work with a student who is deaf and has an interpreter, be sure to talk to the student and not to the interpreter.

- If you work with a student who is blind, talk about what is going on around him or her. For example, "Did you hear the door close? Sally Smith just came into the classroom; she's hanging up her coat."

- As you approach someone who has a dual sensory impairment (deaf-blindness), begin by tapping the person on the shoulder. Move your hand down his or her arm until you reach the hand; then give your identifier. Remember, some students with deaf-blindness often have partial hearing and vision. If that is the case, identify yourself verbally or show them your picture so they know who you are. Be sure to check with the teacher to see if the student already has an established greeting.

- When working with students who are deaf-blind, be sure you are putting your hands underneath their hands rather than grabbing the tops of their hands and manipulating them. This method is called "hand-under-hand" and is much less intrusive.

- When you walk with a student who is blind or deaf-blind, offer your arm to him or her. Watch for and warn about changes in the terrain, transition strips, doorways, etc. At all times you must be aware of your surroundings so you can give the student appropriate directions for navigating the environment.

  Note: You will want to first check with the teacher to ask if you need further training before walking with a student who is blind or deaf-blind.

Notes

Teaching Methodology

Being a peer tutor is a great way to begin learning good special education teaching habits. This section covers important teaching skills and terms to use and remember when serving as a peer tutor.

Prompting

A prompt is a cue that tells special education students what it is you are asking them to do. In the community setting, the prompt or cue can be the sign at the crosswalk that flashes "Don't Walk." In the classroom during a teaching session, the prompt or cue is the teacher or peer tutor giving an instruction—for example, "Give me $4.99," or "What time is it?"

It is important for you to understand how to use prompts, whether working with students in the classroom or out in the community. You also need to know how to determine when prompts are no longer needed and should be faded.

Prompts during Direct Instruction

When teaching a skill in the classroom (direct instruction):

- Make prompts clear. Tell special education students exactly what you want them to do, for example, "Give me $4.99."

- Vary the prompts so that students learn that a variety of cues have the same meaning. For example, you can say "$4.99" or "That will be $4.99."

Prompts in the Real Environment

When teaching a skill in the community (real environment), you will use prompts or cues that occur without your help in that environment. For example, at a street corner, rather than using a verbal prompt of "Stop," point to the "Walk/Don't Walk" sign and say, "That sign says *Walk*; that means go." Or say, "That sign says *Don't Walk*; that means stop or wait."

Fading Prompts

When you are teaching a new skill, your prompts should be frequent and concise. After a student begins to learn a skill in the real environment, give the student the chance to respond on his or her own before prompting for a response. As students learn a skill, the need for prompts is decreased, thus, you can use prompts less frequently—"fading" them.

You will know you have successfully taught a skill when:

- The student responds to natural cues in the community or environment, such as "Walk/Don't Walk" signs.

- The student responds correctly to prompts in the classroom, regardless of how they are presented (for example whether you say, "$4.99," "Give me $4.99," or "$4.99 please," the response is correct).

Notes

Reinforcement

By reinforcing a correct response or behavior, you are increasing the likelihood of the reoccurrence of that behavior. In other words:

BEHAVIOR **>** SOMETHING "GOOD" HAPPENS **>** BEHAVIOR IS LIKELY TO RECUR
(*Reinforcement*)

Types of Reinforcement

It is important to understand that there are different types of reinforcement. You also need to know which reinforcement method is appropriate and when to use it. There are three types of reinforcement: verbal, physical, and tangible.

VERBAL REINFORCEMENT

Verbal reinforcement consists of praise or other words of encouragement. For example, "I like how you are staying on task." Or "You really are working hard!" (See "Pointers for Giving Praise" on page 10.)

PHYSICAL REINFORCEMENT

There are different types of physical reinforcement, and each needs to be age-appropriate. For example, a hug might be appropriate for an elementary-aged student whereas a pat on the back or a "high five" is more natural and acceptable when working with a secondary-aged student.

TANGIBLE REINFORCEMENT

Items that a student can touch or that have value to a special education student can provide tangible reinforcement. Examples of tangible reinforcement can include items such as a paycheck, a token, a '+' on a card, or a certificate of work well done.

Determining the Type of Reinforcement to Use

The appropriate type of reinforcement is often determined by the needs of an individual student or the particular lesson being taught. The type of reinforcement is also often a matter of the preference of an individual tutor or specific special education student. In other words, what works with one student may or may not be effective with another.

You can combine different types of reinforcement. For example, saying "Nice work," while giving a "high five" combines verbal with physical reinforcement.

Frequency of Reinforcement

The frequency of reinforcement is dependent upon where a student is in his or her learning process.

CONTINUOUS REINFORCEMENT

Deliver this method of reinforcement after each and every correct response. Continuous reinforcement is generally used when a student is initially learning a skill.

INTERMITTENT REINFORCEMENT

Deliver this method of reinforcement after a random number of correct responses. Applying intermittent reinforcement is generally used for a student who has learned a skill but still requires feedback about the accuracy of his or her performance.

Delivering Reinforcement

It is vital to the learning process that reinforcement be delivered:

- Immediately
- Clearly
- Frequently

Pointers for Giving Praise

When you praise one of your peer special education students, be specific and encourage the response or behavior you want to see again. Here are some suggestions:

"Nice job...

- paying attention."
- following directions."
- listening to instructions."
- acting like an adult."
- speaking like an adult."
- staying on task."
- working hard."

"I like how you...

- are in your own space."
- are sitting like an adult."
- have your hands and feet to yourself."
- are following directions."
- are listening to directions."
- are trying hard."
- are acting like a high school student."
- are *now* using a quieter tone of voice."

Some Other Words of Praise

- "You're doing a much better job working."
- "That's the way to act like an adult."
- "Thank you for working quietly."
- "I'm so glad you made the right choice."

Notes

Correction Procedures

Using correction procedures appropriately can help increase the skill-levels of special education students as effectively as positive reinforcement does. It is important to use correction procedures so that special education students will learn from their mistakes.

Remember to use correction procedures that are educational rather than harmful to a student's self-esteem.

- Be positive. Avoid saying, "No, that's not right."
- Use steps like these in the following example:
  1. When there is a mistake, say, "Stop" or "Wait," so that the mistake does not continue and become ingrained.
  2. Then say, "Watch me." (Model the behavior, such as: "This is $1.20" and count out the amount.)
  3. Say, "Now you try."
  4. Then reinforce a correct response, such as: "That's right; that is $1.20."

Notes

_____

_____

_____

_____

_____

_____

_____

_____

_____

_____

_____

_____

_____

_____

_____

_____

_____

_____

_____

Summary of Reinforcement and Correction Procedures with Lesson Samples

Remember that:

- When you use reinforcement and correction procedures, both need to be immediate and clear.

- When you give reinforcement, it is the most recent response or behavior that becomes strengthened, especially if that behavior or response is followed with reinforcement in the form of verbal praise.

- Clear and specific praise helps a student understand exactly what he or she has done correctly. For instance, saying "nice job" lets the student know that he did the right thing but does not tell the student what the right thing was. It is better to be specific and say, for example, "Nice job counting out $4.99."

- It might be difficult for you to correct special education students because you do not want to hurt someone's feelings. Be assured, however, that when you use correction procedures appropriately, you are teaching the students you work with—they are learning. When you use clear and appropriate correction procedures, the experience becomes educational rather than ego-deflating for the special education student.

Reinforcement—Lesson Sample

Using reinforcement to teach a skill:

Prompt	Correct Response	Reinforcement
Say, "Give me $4.99."	Student counts out five one-dollar bills.	Say, "Nice job giving me $4.99."

Correction Procedure—Lesson Sample

Using a correction procedure to teach a skill:

Prompt	Response	Correction Procedure
Say, "Give me $4.99."	Student counts, "One, two, four."	When the student makes the mistake, immediately say, "Stop." Repeat the prompt: "$4.99." Say, "Watch me; one, two, three, four, ninety-nine. Now it's your turn."

The correction procedure example shows how the teacher or peer tutor stops the student immediately when the mistake is made or when the number "three" was skipped. Therefore, the student does not learn that four follows two in the sequence. If you do not stop the student at the point of the mistake and he or she keeps counting, the sequence learned is "one, two, four…" rather than "one, two, three, four…"

After stopping the student, you must clearly demonstrate the correct response. For example, "Watch me. This is $4.99" as you count out "one, two, three, four…"

It is natural to want to just say "no," and give the student the correct answer, and then move on to the next trial. However, doing this does not provide the student with the information needed to learn the skill you are trying to teach.

Notes

Data Collection

Data is collected to track student progress and to determine when to move on to the next level of the skill or program.

Teachers use the data to analyze whether to make changes to individual student programs. For example if a student has made little or no progress, it might be time to try a new skill or to break the skill into easier segments. The two methods of data collection most used are:

- Discrete Trial format
- Task Analysis format

Discrete Trial—Recording the Percentage Correct

In the discrete trial data system, you record the correct responses with circles and the incorrect responses with slashes. You are then able to summarize the data by calculating the overall percentage correct over ten to twenty trials of instruction. The dark-edged boxes show the percentage and make a readable "graph" of progress.

Run a minimum of ten trials per day and record for each day that instruction occurs. This is the type of data sheet you will use when teaching skills such as time-telling or counting coins. Here is an example of a discrete trial data sheet with sample data.

Date:	9/1	9/2	9/3											Correct
	10	10	10	10	10	10	10	10	10	10	10	10	10	100%
	9	9	9	9	9	9	9	9	9	9	9	9	9	90%
	8	8	8	8	8	8	8	8	8	8	8	8	8	80%
	7	7	7	7	7	7	7	7	7	7	7	7	7	70%
	6	6	6	6	6	6	6	6	6	6	6	6	6	60%
	5	5	5	5	5	5	5	5	5	5	5	5	5	50%
	4	4	4	4	4	4	4	4	4	4	4	4	4	40%
	3	3	3	3	3	3	3	3	3	3	3	3	3	30%
	2	2	2	2	2	2	2	2	2	2	2	2	2	20%
	1	1	1	1	1	1	1	1	1	1	1	1	1	10%

Prompt: "Give me _____."

Task Analysis—Recording the Number of Prompts

Use the task analysis format to count the number of prompts per step in the process required for a student to perform a particular task or skill. You will teach the skill and record the number of prompts per step until the student can perform the entire task independently.

If a student has difficulty with a particular step, you need to break the task into smaller/simpler steps until the student can perform the task independently. A task analysis is the type of data sheet you will use when you teach skills in the community such as street crossing and grocery shopping.

The following is an example of a task analysis sheet.

Task Analysis		Initials: AB	Initials: AB	Initials:	Initials:	Initials:
		Date: 9/1	Date: 9/4	Date:	Date:	Date:
		Prompts	Prompts	Prompts	Prompts	Prompts
1	Finds nearest bus stop	//	/			
2	Finds bus number	/	/			
3	Gets on correct bus	//	//			
4	Pays/shows pass	/	/			
5	Finds a seat	//	/			
6	Pulls cord prior to stop	/	/			
7	Exits the bus	/	/			
	Total Number of Prompts	10	8			
	Bus Stop Location	3rd & Main	B Street			
	Final Destination	17th St.	J Street			

Accuracy in Data Collection

It is important to understand that you are not "being mean" when you mark responses as incorrect. The rule is: If reinforcing a student's response, the response is marked as correct. However, if you were required to do a correction procedure, the response is marked as incorrect even if the student goes on to respond accurately after having been corrected.

The following diagram illustrates the rule of when to record a response as correct or incorrect.

Prompt ➡ Correct Response ➡ Reinforcement (draw a circle on discrete trial data sheet)

Prompt ➡ Incorrect Response ➡ Correction Procedure (draw a slash on discrete trial data sheet and a hash mark on task analysis data sheets)

Notes

Grade Requirements

To Maintain an "A"

- Spend time with a special education student, three times a term, outside of class time. This can be done in school settings.

- Keep a weekly record using "My Peer Tutor Journal" found in the back of this Handbook. Write about your experiences as a peer tutor working with special education students. Turn in the journal at least three times per semester. The first due date is _____.

- Educate at least one of your peers about disabilities. Explain to the special education teacher how you accomplished this.

To Maintain a "B"

- Spend time with a special education student, two times a term, outside of class time.

- Keep a weekly record using "My Peer Tutor Journal" found in the back of this Handbook. Write about your experiences as a peer tutor working with special education students. Turn in the journal at least three times per semester. The first due date is _____.

- Educate at least one of your peers about disabilities. Explain to the special education teacher how you accomplished this.

To Maintain a "C"

- Work with special education students in class.

- Keep a weekly record using "My Peer Tutor Journal" found in the back of this Handbook. Write about your experiences as a peer tutor working with special education students. Turn in the journal at least three times per semester. The first due date is _____.

- Educate at least one of your peers about disabilities. Explain to the special education teacher how you accomplished this.

When asked what he'd gained from his peer tutor experience, Joel said, "A bunch of great friends and life experiences I will never forget."

Amanda said, "I became a peer tutor because I've always wanted to work in the special education field and I wanted to gain experience and joy from working with great kids."

Weekly Planner

SEPTEMBER

WEEK 1

Monday _____

Tuesday _____

Wednesday _____

Thursday _____

Friday _____

WEEK 2

Monday _____

Tuesday _____

Wednesday _____

Thursday _____

Friday _____

WEEK 3

Monday _____

Tuesday _____

Wednesday _____

Thursday _____

Friday _____

WEEK 4

Monday _____

Tuesday _____

Wednesday _____

Thursday _____

Friday _____

OCTOBER

WEEK 1

Monday _____

Tuesday _____

Wednesday _____

Thursday _____

Friday _____

WEEK 2

Monday _____

Tuesday _____

Wednesday _____

Thursday _____

Friday _____

WEEK 3

Monday _____

Tuesday _____

Wednesday _____

Thursday _____

Friday _____

WEEK 4

Monday _____

Tuesday _____

Wednesday _____

Thursday _____

Friday _____

NOVEMBER

WEEK 1

Monday _____

Tuesday _____

Wednesday _____

Thursday _____

Friday _____

WEEK 2

Monday _____

Tuesday _____

Wednesday _____

Thursday _____

Friday _____

WEEK 3

Monday _____

Tuesday _____

Wednesday _____

Thursday _____

Friday _____

WEEK 4

Monday _____

Tuesday _____

Wednesday _____

Thursday _____

Friday _____

DECEMBER

WEEK 1

Monday

Tuesday

Wednesday

Thursday

Friday

WEEK 2

Monday

Tuesday

Wednesday

Thursday

Friday

WEEK 3

Monday

Tuesday

Wednesday

Thursday

Friday

WEEK 4

Monday

Tuesday

Wednesday

Thursday

Friday

JANUARY

WEEK 1

Monday _____

Tuesday _____

Wednesday _____

Thursday _____

Friday _____

WEEK 2

Monday _____

Tuesday _____

Wednesday _____

Thursday _____

Friday _____

WEEK 3

Monday _____

Tuesday _____

Wednesday _____

Thursday _____

Friday _____

WEEK 4

Monday _____

Tuesday _____

Wednesday _____

Thursday _____

Friday _____

FEBRUARY

WEEK 1

Monday	
Tuesday	
Wednesday	
Thursday	
Friday	

WEEK 2

Monday	
Tuesday	
Wednesday	
Thursday	
Friday	

WEEK 3

Monday	
Tuesday	
Wednesday	
Thursday	
Friday	

WEEK 4

Monday	
Tuesday	
Wednesday	
Thursday	
Friday	

MARCH

WEEK 1

Monday _____

Tuesday _____

Wednesday _____

Thursday _____

Friday _____

WEEK 2

Monday _____

Tuesday _____

Wednesday _____

Thursday _____

Friday _____

WEEK 3

Monday _____

Tuesday _____

Wednesday _____

Thursday _____

Friday _____

WEEK 4

Monday _____

Tuesday _____

Wednesday _____

Thursday _____

Friday _____

APRIL

WEEK 1

Monday	
Tuesday	
Wednesday	
Thursday	
Friday	

WEEK 2

Monday	
Tuesday	
Wednesday	
Thursday	
Friday	

WEEK 3

Monday	
Tuesday	
Wednesday	
Thursday	
Friday	

WEEK 4

Monday	
Tuesday	
Wednesday	
Thursday	
Friday	

MAY

WEEK 1

Monday	_____
Tuesday	_____
Wednesday	_____
Thursday	_____
Friday	_____

WEEK 2

Monday	_____
Tuesday	_____
Wednesday	_____
Thursday	_____
Friday	_____

WEEK 3

Monday	_____
Tuesday	_____
Wednesday	_____
Thursday	_____
Friday	_____

WEEK 4

Monday	_____
Tuesday	_____
Wednesday	_____
Thursday	_____
Friday	_____

JUNE

WEEK 1

Monday	
Tuesday	
Wednesday	
Thursday	
Friday	

WEEK 2

Monday	
Tuesday	
Wednesday	
Thursday	
Friday	

WEEK 3

Monday	
Tuesday	
Wednesday	
Thursday	
Friday	

WEEK 4

Monday	
Tuesday	
Wednesday	
Thursday	
Friday	

My Peer Tutor Journal

Date:

Date:

Date:

Date:

Date:

Date:

Date:

Date:

Date:

Date:

Date:

Date:

Date:

Date:

Date:

Date:

Date:

_____

_____

_____

_____

_____

_____

Date:

_____

_____

_____

_____

_____

_____

Date:

_____

_____

_____

_____

_____

_____

Date:

_____

_____

_____

_____

_____

Date:

Date:

Date:

Date:

Date:

_____

_____

_____

_____

_____

Date:

_____

_____

_____

_____

_____

Date:

_____

_____

_____

_____

_____

Date:

_____

_____

_____

_____

_____

Date:

Date:

Date:

Date:

Date:

Date:

Date:

Date:

Date:

Date:

Date:

Date:

Made in the USA
Columbia, SC
21 August 2024

40762819R00050